D1328289

The Spirit of St. Francisville

Paradise in the Felicianas

Darrell Chitty

Anne Butler

Library of Congress Cataloging in Publication Data
Chitty, Darrell
ISBN# 0-9763765-9-8
Printed in China

Table of Contents

Introduction
Let's get one thing straight right from the start.

This is NOT a tourist guide. Oh, sure, it includes lots of the sights visitors won't want to miss and lots of the events they'll want to include on their itinerary. But this book is a whole lot more, because it doesn't stop at the surface. Through his astute choice of subjects, his very personal and fond focus, his amazingly creative compositions and his technical skill, prize-winning Louisiana professional photographer Darrell Chitty opens a window into the very soul of this special place called St. Francisville, showing us the substance, the meaning, the true heart.

And let's get one more thing straight, while we're at it.

Darrell Chitty is not just a photographer. He's an artist. Which is not to say that other fine photographers are not artists as well, but Darrell Chitty is...how shall we say it...truly a painter without a paintbrush. Instead of canvas and paint pots, Darrell creates impressionistic masterpieces by painting with camera and computer, combining his modern technological skills with an abiding appreciation and in-depth knowledge of art history and the age-old techniques of the Old Masters. The consummate professional, twice named Louisiana Photographer of the Year, he conducts seminars and workshops, and has his

5

own studio, his own art gallery, and a following of admirers and patrons around the world.

The superb photographs in this book represent but a smattering of the sturdy salient souls whose special contributions, both great and small, have mattered in the life of the little rivertown of St. Francisville in that part of Louisiana long called Feliciana, the Happy Land. This is not an all-inclusive directory of residents or residences; it's merely a random representative sampling, just enough to whet the reader's appetite by providing a tantalizing glimpse of the spirit of St. Francisville.

Like all small towns, St. Francisville has its share of faults, not the least of which is that gossip can travel from one end of town to the other faster than a speeding bullet. But this is not just any small town, it's a Southern small town. And in Southern small towns, faults often stroll happily hand-in-hand with virtues, and if the news is bad, before it reaches the opposite end of town there are ten kindly old ladies rushing up the front-porch steps bearing fresh-baked buttermilk pies or shrimp-crawfish casseroles to cushion the blow and console the recipient of ill tidings. Can that kind of caring be shown in a photograph? You bet it can; just take a look and you'll see it on every page.

Artist, accomplished musician, boatbuilder, world traveller, scholar, dreamer...Darrell Chitty is uniquely qualified to reproduce the amazing vision showcased in this incredible book. Because, you see, anybody can see the surface. It takes an artist to see the soul.

--Anne Butler--

Butler Greenwood Plantation

The River

The Giver of Life

Of course the story has to start with the river, the Father of Waters, the Mighty Mississippi, for it is St. Francisville's proximity to the river that has most markedly shaped its development and its destiny. The river was the giver of life, watering, fertilizing, enriching. And the river brought destruction as well, when the roaring torrents of springtime swept away all in their path. And then the cycle began anew, the floodwaters depositing rich nutrients, the land drying to renewed fertility, life sprouting once again to thrive until the next flood season.

The river's currents shaped the land, high bluffs along much of the eastern bank overlooking the flat fertile bottom lands along the western so that the wealthy planters from Natchez to St. Francisville in the antebellum days lived on the high side and often planted on the low. But before the planters, the river saw the slim silent canoes of the earliest residents, the peaceable Houma Indians and then the fierce Tunica tribe. They must have watched in awe as the first European explorers appeared on these waters. LaSalle, the French explorer claiming Louisiana and the Mississippi Valley for France, first mentions the Houma Indians living along the banks of the Mississippi River in 1682. Chevalier Henri de Tonti found the "Oumas tribe, the bravest of all the savages," and in 1699 Iberville also met the great "Chef des Oumas" and gave him some apple and cotton seeds. The explorers gave the Indians European-made trade goods; they also gave them dysentery and diseases against which they had no immunity.

Soon along the waters came the earliest pioneers, the traders and trappers and adventurers, their flatboats loaded with produce and goods, drifting with the current to New Orleans, where the goods were sold, the boats were broken up and used for lumber, and the boatmen set out afoot for home upriver.

The calm waters of Bayou Sara, emptying into the Mississippi River just below the bluffs upon which St. Francisville developed, provided a safe anchorage for these flatboats, and there a rowdy riverside port city called Bayou Sara soon sprang up, its saloons and gambling dens and brothels catering to the randy needs of the boatmen. Like the similar riverbank shantytown of Natchez-

River of Riches

Under-the-Hill, it was said that for a time here the only thing cheaper than a woman's body was a man's life. King of the flatboatmen, of course, was the legendary Mike Fink, who boasted, "I can outrun, out hop, throw down, drag out and lick any man in the country. I'm a salt-river roarer, I am; I love the wimming and I'm chock full of fight."

As early as the 1780's the District of Feliciana was attracting mainly Anglo-American settlers, recipients of Spanish landgrants drawn by the long growing seasons and gentle climate and rolling landscapes reminiscent of homes remembered in Virginia or Pennsylvania or the Carolinas, England, Ireland or Scotland, and development began in earnest as the area went from French to English to Spanish and then finally American rule.

Atop the hill St. Francisville was actually a burial ground, the Capuchin friars from French Pointe Coupee Parish crossing the river to inter their dead on lands safe from the floodwaters. By 1807 the town of St. Francisville was chartered, its name taken from the patron saint of the monks and its development plotted along a narrow loessial finger ridge restricting development to a single main street and short side street, so that it was called "the town two miles long and two yards wide."

Soon the lower reaches of the Mississippi would be called the River of Riches, its banks lined with immense indigo, cotton and sugar plantations where vast fortunes were made. And along the river waters came the fabulous floating palaces called steamboats, transporting the plantation aristocracy in style to the lively social season and the center of business in New Orleans, piled high with their bales of cotton and hogsheads of sugar bound for factors in the Crescent City for sale to markets east and west, then transporting back to the plantations

the fine furnishings and fancy goods purchased in the city and abroad, often on credit against the crop, to enhance life in the country.

Bayou Sara

In its glory days before the Civil War, Bayou Sara was one of the largest ports on the Mississippi River between New Orleans and Memphis. A mile of brick warehouses lined the waterfront to store cotton awaiting shipment to New Orleans. Fast packets and fanciful steamboats pulled up to the banks to disgorge passengers and deliveries as sweating roustabouts piled bales so high around the sides that the boats themselves all but disappeared from view. The extensive residential sections of Bayou Sara had elaborate homes for the prosperous merchants, and the bustling commercial district boasted fine hotels and livery stables, saloons and emporiums peddling goods shipped in from around the world; even some of the nation's finest cabinetmakers had outlets to provide custom furnishings for the magnificent plantation houses being erected in the surrounding countryside. Bayou Sara had boarding houses, drugstores and apothecaries, saw mills and lumber yards, livestock traders and butchers, fish markets, fairgrounds, baseball fields, grocers and dry-goods stores, post and express offices, clothiers, ice houses and banks.

It also had, just at its outskirts, the terminus for the country's first standard gauge railroad, chartered in 1831 as a feeder line to haul the all-important cotton crop from the highly productive plantations in southwest Mississippi and Louisiana to the bustling port at Bayou Sara. Track was laid for 27 miles, the crude rails of wood capped with thin strips of iron, and construction cost $25,000 per mile. Bayou Sara town fathers feared this screeching, belching "iron horse" and refused to let it enter town limits, and before long it would be the railroads that eventually superseded the steamboats so that commercial traffic bypassed the little river ports like Bayou Sara. But there were more immediate problems directly around the bend.

Both a blessing and a curse

Bayou Sara was laid out on flat land right beside the riverbanks, and the river was its blessing and the river was its curse. The river enriched, fertilized, transported. But as it gave, it also took away. The steamboats with their overheated boilers blew up midstream, flinging flaming passengers into the roiling waves. And each spring the river swelled with melted snow and rain, turning into raging

torrents bursting through crevasses in the flimsy levees erected privately by individual planters and farmers, inundating surrounding areas with ten or twenty feet of water, sweeping away crops and cattle and entire communities, half-submerged houses floating down river with whole families clinging precariously to peaked roofs.

Only the ferry landing remains

In 1927 the river flooded 26,000 square miles and left over 600,000 people homeless and huddled in Red Cross tent cities along the lower Mississippi, the most extensive flood in the history of the country and the incentive to implement serious coordinated levee control. Bayou Sara was obliterated, a few of its sturdier structures hauled up the hill to St. Francisville behind teams of straining oxen; there's nothing left of this once-thriving little riverport at all today, except the ferry landing. Atop the hill, St. Francisville became the prosperous center of commerce and culture for the rich surrounding plantation country.

13

Through the centuries, to the banks of the river came the dreamers, the visionaries, gazing at the swift current and dreaming of what the river could give them, the adventures, the travels, the untold riches. And sometimes the river did give those things. But also to the river came the mourners, grieving for what the river took away, the lives, the loves, the lands. And the river did take those things as well. The river was gentle and generous in some seasons, and in others the river was greedy, hungry, voracious. And through the centuries, the pattern repeated itself; the river kept right on giving, right on taking, right on rolling, rolling, rolling along.

The Land

As much as the river shaped the development of the area, so did the land, for it was a terrain unique in what would become the state of Louisiana.

It was the terrain, the hills and hollows so different from the flat bottom lands and tangled fetid swamps on the other side of the river, that influenced who the early settlers would be. It was also the terrain that influenced what crops would best be cultivated here, indigo and then cotton rather than the waving fields of sugar cane grown farther south and west.

But first, it was the land that supported the rich abundance of wild game that watered at the river's banks and along the creeks and tributaries emptying into it, following the same familiar track through thick brush to water holes and feeding grounds and the Mississippi River. Soon the prehistoric game trails had been stamped into footpaths by the moccasin-clad feet of Indian hunters, their stealthy passage breaking only briefly the primeval silence of the dense forest.

The footpaths became rude narrow roads and the forests echoed with the sound of an endless succession of hooves: the herds of wild mustangs driven from Texas and Mexico on horse-hunting expeditions, then the plodding burros and pack animals carrying supplies for trappers and adventurous explorers. Before long these early roads were deeply rutted with wagon tracks as heavy draft horses hauled covered wagons and stagecoaches full of pioneers and supplies. Over the roads tireless sturdy mules and oxen dragged felled timbers for building fine homes and pulled bales of cotton to landings along the river for shipment to commission merchants in New Orleans to finance those same fine homes.

Then came the high-stepping smooth-gaited walking horses favored by the planters surveying their endless cotton fields, and the blooded thoroughbreds in training to run on plantation racetracks with fortunes wagered on the outcome, and the matched bays with sleek shiny coats prancing before carriages and fine coaches full of Feliciana folk visiting from one isolated plantation home to another on visits which sometimes lasted months. There were also the fleet ponies of the bandits and highwaymen armed with cutlasses and pistols to prey upon the honest travelers along the old trace roads. One early historian reported that "many an old Negro teamster, sent from the inland plantations with money to buy produce of all kinds from the flatboats tied up at Bayou Sara, would be made to stand and deliver, and would return home with chattering teeth, empty pockets and wagon after an encounter with them." With every footstep the roadbeds were imprinted just a little deeper into this uniquely soft loessial soil. Sections of original early roads that remain today, like the sunken Old Tunica Road, have sides towering dozens of feet above the well-traveled trace, the overhanging trees atop the bluffs forming a shady canopy like a thick tunnel.

Biologists and botanists consider the Tunica Hills one of the most biologically rich regions in Louisiana, providing habitat for the threatened Louisiana black bear, southern unstriped scorpion, Webster's salamander and eastern chipmunk; the latter two live nowhere else in the state. Experts also consider the Tunica Hills to have a wider variety of trees than any other forest in the continental United States, and there are dozens of rare plant species, including the shadow-witch orchid, pyramid magnolia, Indian tobacco, enchanter's nightshade, fairy wand, climbing bittersweet, glade fern, Canada wild ginger, wild baneberry, silvery glade fern, lowland brittle fern, Allegheny spurge, Southern shield wood fern, Nodding pogonia, low erythrodes and ginseng.

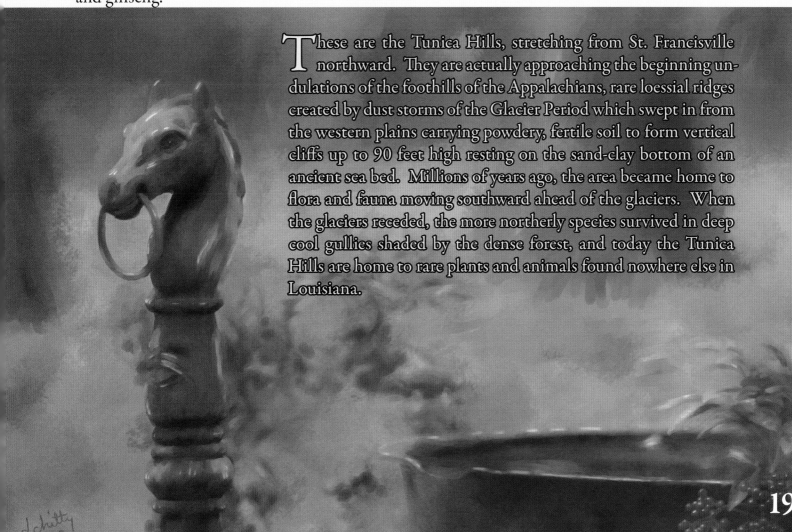

These are the Tunica Hills, stretching from St. Francisville northward. They are actually approaching the beginning undulations of the foothills of the Appalachians, rare loessial ridges created by dust storms of the Glacier Period which swept in from the western plains carrying powdery, fertile soil to form vertical cliffs up to 90 feet high resting on the sand-clay bottom of an ancient sea bed. Millions of years ago, the area became home to flora and fauna moving southward ahead of the glaciers. When the glaciers receded, the more northerly species survived in deep cool gullies shaded by the dense forest, and today the Tunica Hills are home to rare plants and animals found nowhere else in Louisiana.

Audubon-inspired artist, Murrell Butler, still explores the magical scenery of Feliciana as shown in these two paintings.

With habitat areas ranging from the hilly loessial bluffs and steep shady ravines of the uplands to the swampy river bottomlands and hardwood forests, birdwatchers find the area still teems with the same rich abundance of birdlife that so inspired the artist Audubon in the 1820's. Besides providing year-round habitat for such interesting specimens as the Cooper's hawk, worm-eating warbler, Louisiana waterthrush and white-breasted nuthatch, the hills host dozens of species of neotropical breeding migrants which winter further south in Latin America.

Today Cat Island National Wildlife Refuge preserves one of the largest tracts of virgin wetland forest along the Mississippi River not protected by levees from cyclical flooding. Sometimes inundated by 15 to 20 feet of water in the spring, Cat Island supports huge populations of wintering waterfowl, as well as the world's largest bald cypress tree, believed to be 800 to 1500 years old and an astounding 85 feet tall.

Tunica Hills Wildlife Management Area has 6,000 acres of rugged hills, high bluffs and deep shaded ravines sheltering a significant wealth of rare plant and animal species. A 635-acre Tunica Hills State Preservation Area encompassing bluffs and bayous and interpretive centers is planned to tell the story of the early Tunica Indians and the later Civil War battle at nearby Como Landing, while introducing Louisiana's "flatlanders" to this hilly unspoiled site. Best way to experience the wonders of this pristine wilderness area, little changed from the time the early settlers first marvelled at its spectacular beauty, is on foot or on one of Cross Creek Stables' gaited horses.

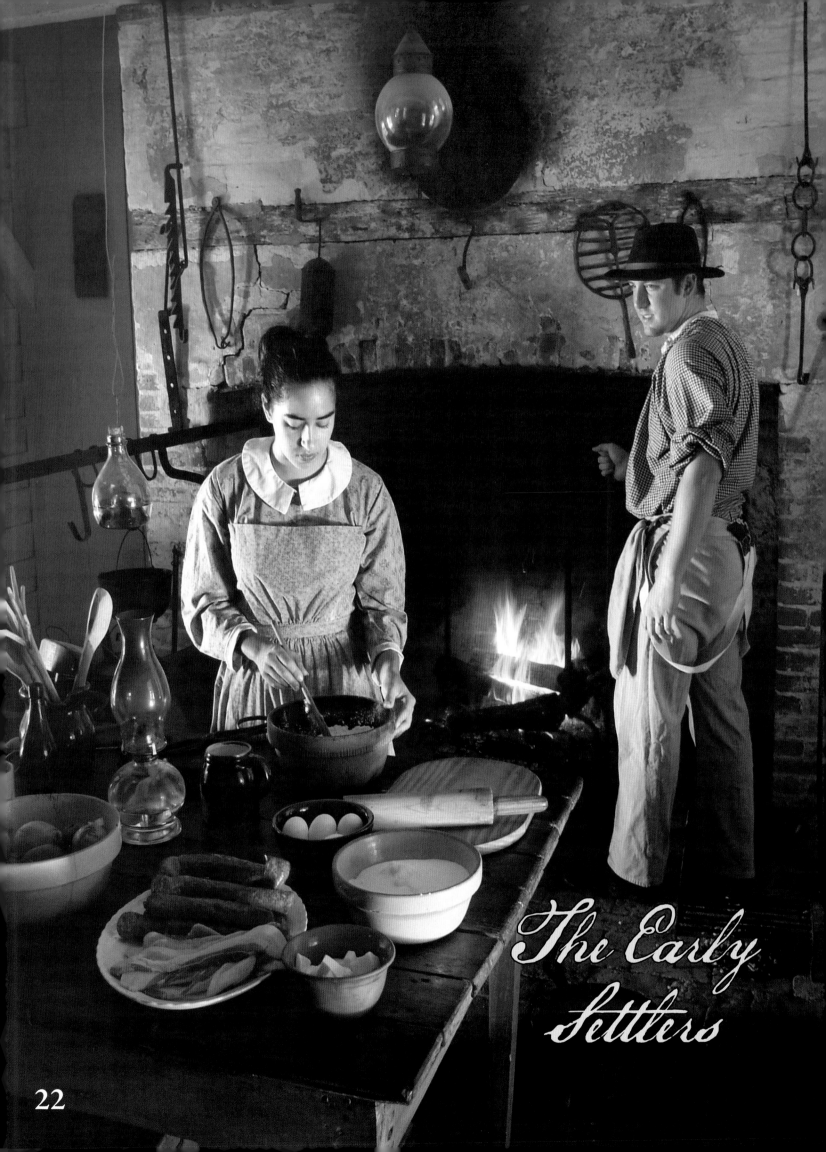

The Early Settlers

They were a hardy and courageous bunch, these early Anglo settlers who migrated down from the East Coast, mostly from Pennsylvania and Virginia and the Carolinas, to start new lives in this new territory that was English and then Spanish.

Some, like widowed Olivia Ruffin Barrow, travelled by wagon train and then riverboat, accompanied by grown sons and daughters, trunks full of fine clothing and treasured household furnishings, and the skilled slaves who would build the simple but elegant home on Highland Plantation along Little Bayou Sara as the center of a family dynasty that saw, in future generations, the building of such magnificent plantations as Greenwood, Rosebank, Ellerslie, Afton Villa and Rosedown.

Another early pioneer, Samuel Flower of Butler Greenwood Plantation, was married, so it says in florid script on the original wax-sealed wedding certificate displayed today in his home, according to the rites of the Church of England but "without benefit of clergy," the services performed by the wagon master as he travelled through Virginia on his way from Pennsylvania; once he arrived in Louisiana, he used his medical skills to improve life in this new territory where yellow fever and other rapidly spreading plagues wiped out whole generations at a time, and even treated the wife of the Spanish governor. Judge Thomas Butler of The Cottage was the first judge in the Florida Parishes, typical of the early settlers who, besides planting extensive acreage, quickly assumed substantial roles in the development of the area, as judges, magistrates, congressmen.

Some of those who came down in this early English migration were Tories, English sympathizers during the Revolutionary War; on the other hand, Dr. Flower's brother hid the Liberty Bell from the British in Pennsylvania, and the Butlers of The Cottage Plantation all fought valiantly with George Washington for American freedom, as did David Bradford of The Myrtles. Regardless of roles in the Revolutionary War, these were substantial folk; the third English governor of West Florida remarked that his district contained a unusually large number of respectable wealthy planters, practical souls who came to cultivate the soil but brought with them an abundance of capital as well as a full measure of energy and intelligence. And a young military man, visiting the area in the 1790's from his home in Pennsylvania, remarked that, to his "utter astonishment, I found a number of exceedingly genteel people...all rich...(and) as many handsome and accomplished women as I ever saw in my life."

In the Felicianas they found rolling hills and deep hollows that reminded them of home; they found a felicitous semi-tropical climate with long growing seasons, plentiful water supplies, rich fertile soil, and they set about clearing the fields and planting. Their first important cash crop was the indigo used to make blue dye, a valuable commodity, and much of it was sold on contract to the Prussian Army to color the uniforms. But cyanide also was made from the indigo plant, and the mortality rate among the labor force proved unacceptably high. Cotton quickly supplanted indigo as the economic mainstay of the plantation culture, particularly after Eli Whitney's cotton gin perfected the process of mechanically removing all those troublesome seeds from each boll, previously a time-consuming task done by hand, and soon vast stacks of bales were piled in warehouses along the Mississippi River at Bayou Sara awaiting shipment.

The cotton empire existed rather precariously on credit, with planters borrowing against future crops as needed, some years making vast profits, some years barely breaking even, and some years living on credit and the faith that next year's crop and market and weather would all be better.

An influx of Jewish immigrants in the mid-1800's, escaping religious persecution in the Old Country, followed the westward movement of the cotton empire, their mercantile skills proving invaluable in the agrarian South. All along the Mississippi River, including Bayou Sara and St. Francisville, Jewish tradesmen operated many of the drygoods stores and other businesses supporting the plantation empire, providing credit when needed, building cotton gins and presses, dabbling in real estate, and when they took crops as payment, they found themselves in the cotton business as much as any planter.

The southern plantation system was built on slave labor. The St. Francisville Chronicle reported statistics from the tax rolls of 1853 showing that the parish of West Feliciana, with St. Francisville at its core, contained 2,231 free whites, 70 free blacks and 10,298 slaves, who produced in that year 2,873 hogsheads of sugar, 4,318 barrels of molasses, 334,000 bushels of corn and 23,860 bales of cotton selling at about $70 a bale. Some plantations, like William Ruffin Barrow's Greenwood, had as many as 750 slaves to till his 12,000 acres.

A number of the slaves on every plantation were skilled artisans, blacksmiths and builders, tanners and wheelwrights, furniture makers, gardeners, accomplished seamstresses, spinners and weavers.

In the outside kitchens, detached from the main houses because of heat and fire danger, not to mention clatter and noise, many a black cook flavored the bland old English cuisine with the spice of a Caribbean or African heritage, the okra and peppers and other secret ingredients making vast improvements in taste. Plantation records were itemized and detailed; the records from Rosedown, year by year, inventoried household furnishings and equipment ("24 soup plates, 1 large sugar spoon with holes, 6 nut crackers, and 12 nut picks, 2 pickle knives...5 coloured counterpains, 3 featherbeds, 49 damask towels altogether...11 flowered finger bowls and 13 dark blue...etc."), animals ("40 sheep, 2 bulls 1 old and 1 young, 6 oxen") and the labor force as well ("little negroes 105, hands 248, no accounts 12").

Everything the Family Needed

On isolated self-sufficient plantations, nearly everything the family needed could be supplied right on the place, with only periodic trips to town to purchase a few staples, and so the slaves and the plantation mistresses as well became skilled at an amazing number of task

The men bred fine horseflesh and in some cases had their own racetracks, as at Rosedown Plantation and Greenwood. They kept birddogs and hunting hounds, supplying the table with a bounty of wild game; they fished in the river and lakes, the Barrows even keeping their own river steamer, and ordered fresh oysters sent up from the coast by steamboat. They raised herds of cattle and hogs and sheep, for meat and butter and milk, for hides to tan and wool to spin into yarn. Flocks of poultry were raised for food and feathers to stuff mattresses, and sometimes there were exotic fowl like peacocks raised simply to add beauty.

There were huge gardens of vegetables and the herbs used for culinary and medical purposes, and orchards of fruit trees. Smokehouses cured the hams and sausages so they could last throughout the year, and other meats were pickled or cured in brine. Big circular brick-lined underground root cellars, like the one still to be seen at Butler Greenwood Plantation, provided cool storage for root crops and other commodities, and pantries and commissaries like the one still standing on The Cottage Plantation were stocked with barrels of molasses, hogsheads of sugar, hampers of potatoes and apples, casks or demijohns of wines and other supplies.

Meal was ground from corn, and some of the plantations like Greenwood and Highland had their own sugar and syrup mills as well as gristmills.

Not everyone lived on a plantation

Not everyone lived on these self-sufficient plantation communities, of course; there were small farmers and a growing population of townsfolk, though even in 1853 the tax rolls listed only 55 persons as having trades or professions. But even in tiny St. Francisville, improvements were quickly effected. By 1809 a hotel had been erected; the Louisiana Territory's third newspaper was established and its editor became the first American war correspondent covering the War of 1812. The second library in the state began in 1812 in St. Francisville, a Masonic Lodge was chartered in 1817, and by 1828 the

state's first Episcopal congregation outside New Orleans had joined together in worship at Grace Church, the vestry and congregation comprised of the early Anglo plantation patriarchs, the Barrows, the Butlers, the Forts and Bowmans, the Flowers, the Stirlings and the like.

It would not be long before these enterprising and strongwilled early settlers would chafe under Spanish rule, particularly when this eastern side of the river continued to be claimed by Spain as part of West Florida and was excluded from the Louisiana Purchase of 1803 as President Thomas Jefferson acquired, at the bargain price of $15,000,000 or 4 cents an acre, the entire central third of the country including New Orleans, essentially doubling the size of the fledgling United States. In 1804 an abortive rebellion gained less than universal support among the planters, its organizers, the rough and rowdy Kemper brothers, seen as true patriots by some and as renegade outlaws by others. John Mills, the founder of Bayou Sara, wrote of being accosted by one of the brothers, "a rifle gun & long knife sticking at his breast, a pistol sticking in the waistband of his breeches, and a dagger hanging at his side," and another who crossed the Kempers had his ears cut off "with a dull knife" and displayed, pickled in wine, at the family tavern.

The seeds of resistance had been sown, although it would not be until six years later that the residents of West Florida would rise up against the Spanish government in a successful rebellion precipitated by international and local changes... the death of the Spanish king, Napoleon's invasion of Spain, a deterioration of relations with local Spanish officials stemming from the Kemper raids, more restrictive land acquisition policies. By 1810, the Anglo residents of Feliciana in Spanish West Florida were ready to become Americans. They drew together in secret and made elaborate plans for the Republic of West Florida, complete with carefully thought out constitution, militia and duly elected government. Inspired by such leaders as William Barrow of Highland and Lewis Stirling of Wakefield Plantation, the planters successfully overthrew the Spanish regime and set up their own free and independent state, its capital in St. Francisville. The revolt lasted 74 days. Then the Republic of West Florida joined the Union along with the rest of Louisiana to become a state in 1812.

The Homes They Built

S t. Francisville is now a year-round tourist destination, its peaceful thoroughfares shaded by ancient live oaks, the glorious galleries of its Victorian homes dripping with gingerbread, its main street still the viable center of life, and its entire downtown area a National Register Historic District attesting to its architectural and historical significance.

But its early streets were muddy, rutted tracks down which cattle were driven en route to the river or railroad, wagonloads of cotton or corn were hauled to the cotton gins and gristmills, and sporadic raised boardwalks provided dry passage for patrons of the drygoods emporiums and other mercantile establishments. The early townsfolk prospered and built homes that were ever more substantial, adding on to simple core structures as families grew and needs expanded, but it was in the countryside that the antebellum plantation culture blossomed into a veritable garden of admirable architecture.

When the Spanish government used land grants in the late 1700's to stabilize the area, they lured well-established Anglo-Saxons from the eastern seaboard, who came down with large family groups and the means to start and stick with the early plantations. Not for them were the Creole or French-influenced structures seen farther to the south along the River Road, raised high to escape the threat of floodwaters. These Feliciana settlers built structures reminiscent of their own earlier homes, English cottage-style plantation homes with adaptations to suit the southern climate...high ceilings, double French doors or floor-to-ceiling windows providing plenty of cross ventilation, and broad surrounding galleries that shaded the interiors and made life bearable in the hot, humid summers.

The earliest plantations in the area date mostly from the 1790's, when the first valiant efforts were made to tame the virgin woodlands and till the rich river bottom lands into vast fields of indigo and cotton, prospering sufficiently

that the planters along the Great River Road from New Orleans to Natchez comprised a large percentage of America's mid-1800's millionaires. The houses they built reflected their status, although the earliest homes were more practical than pretentious. Cypress trees and blue poplar for framing and building were cut and aged on the plantations, turned into lumber with water-powered sawmills as was done at Wakefield Plantation, or shipped upriver to Cincinnati for milling. The solid joists and mortised beams, hewn by hand, were joined by wooden pegs and hand-wrought nails; shingles for roofing were rived by hand with froes from cypress logs and clay bricks for piers and hearths and chimneys were fired in kilns on the spot.

Interior house walls were slim strips of cypress lathing plastered over with fine river silt and white animal hair in the refined English method (not the rough bousillage combining mud and moss and deer hair utilized in other areas). By the mid-1800's these walls were being embellished with elaborate plaster moldings and

ceiling medallions from which hung magnificent chandeliers whose candles and reflective crystals brightened dark interiors.

Surrounding the main houses were a multitude of dependencies, barns and corncribs, stables and smithies, commissaries and kitchens, school houses, law offices and doctor's offices, chicken coops, smokehouses, laundry rooms and slave quarters. The Cottage and Rosedown Plantations have the largest collections of extant outbuildings, providing a clear understanding of how the plantation communities functioned. Oakley Plantation also has fascinating early dependencies, and the original outside kitchen at Butler Greenwood, dating from the 1790's, is one of the few structures left showing early Spanish architectural influences.

In the midst of the wilderness, the plantations were isolated enclaves of culture, with European tutors in residence to educate the children until the boys at least were old enough to be sent to colleges Up East or abroad, and music or dancing masters engaged periodically. When planting seasons permitted, the families traveled extensively; being right on the Mississippi River, they could get to New Orleans and thence around the world with comparative ease, and they did, enjoying the social seasons at all the most fashionable wateringholes. As they traveled, they selected fine furnishings and handpainted china, Italian marbles and French porcelains, Belgian carpets and other embellishments to be shipped back home. Soon polished mahogany dining tables and carved sideboards groaned with the weight of finely executed silver services and sets of china with hundreds of pieces. Formal parlors like the one at Butler Greenwood Plantation had matching sets of rosewood furniture and damask lambrequins at the windows, floral Brussels carpet on the floor and fine family oil portraits lining the walls.

Music rooms were fitted out with great gilded harps and violins, flutes and the French Pleyel pianos that Chopin favored; at Catalpa, Mrs. Fort was blind in her old age but took solace in music, literally wearing the ivory off the piano keys. The ladies excelled at playing these instruments to entertain guests and visiting dignitaries, like the Grand Duke Alexis of Russia and General Andrew Jackson on his way home from the Battle of New Orleans, both of whom enjoyed the hospitality of The Cottage Plantation. Miss Louise Butler of The Cottage, turn-of-the-century historian and contributor of scholarly pieces to the Louisiana Historical Quarterly, remembered these musical evenings: "on summer evenings long and long ago, there floated out on the scented night air, sweet melodies, interwoven with moon and star beams, and in that romance-breathing entourage the charm was as ravishing as when Paganini played

or Garcia sang. Later on, one family had an entire string band from New Orleans for the whole summer. It played for them and their guests, but the delightful sounds reached the neighbors half a mile away..."

Each family had its treasured "family plate," elaborate silver service with repousse decoration consisting of coffee pot, teapot, sugar dish, creamer, and what was commonly referred to, rather vulgarly, as the slop bowl, used to dump the old tea leaves when pots and cups were replenished with fresh tea. Set upon heavy richly embellished trays, these silver services were often skillfully crafted in England or on the East Coast, though some were New Orleans silver. That they made it across the ocean or down the river and through several generations of servants polishing with none too careful hands was remarkable, but even more remarkable was their survival of the Civil War, when pillaging troops made off with many family heirlooms. Some of the more savvy mistresses buried their silver in ponds, as they did at Catalpa Plantation, or beneath camellia bushes as at Butler Green-wood Plantation, so that the silver made it through the war with only minor dents and scratches to be passed down through yet more generations.

Libraries were filled with leather-bound first editions of all the great classics, and the bedrooms were crowded with magnificent four-posters draped with the all-important protective mosquito bars. The families visited relatives on plantations up and down the Mississippi, the visits sometimes lasting for months, and when they married, it was mostly among the same group of plantation families.

Miss Louise Butler recounted a typical family visit, the guest arriving "in the family coach which was usually upholstered in soft grey broadcloth, as the owners had too much pride to be ostentatious, and was provided with embroidered straps by which to hang, for roads were rough and the vehicle swung high on prodigious springs, so the lurching was frightful and the occupants usually reached their destination suffering from mal de mer, slight to violent, according to their powers of endurance." Not to worry; the seasick new arrivals were quickly fortified with cordials, juleps, claret, sherry, punch, champagne and coffee with spirits, so that "the gentlemen, especially, departed with eyes considerably brighter than when they arrived." The dinner would have been superb, and the punch, says this early historian, was proudly ladled from the enormous family punch bowl of fine china or cut glass, "as mammy often said, 'big ernuff to swim de baby, effen he tuck his baff in hit.'" The guests were always welcomed with true southern hospitality, even, according to Miss Louise Butler, the poor relations and "the Old Soak, of which species every family condoned at least one."

Some of the area's early plantation manors have tragically been lost. Trudeau has deteriorated irreparably through neglect, Oakland and Woodlawn, Waverly and Solitaire all burned to the ground, and so did Greenwood Plantation, but it was lucky enough to be raised from the ashes. The Gothic castle of a main house called Afton Villa was also lost to fire, but its ruins have been adaptively utilized as the foundation for a glorious garden. Fortunately, other early plantation houses remain, some like Highland and Butler Greenwood incredibly still in the original families, still family homes.

Six of these plantations are open to the public for daily tours, presenting a fascinating glimpse of life in the formative years of the area. At the two state properties, Rosedown and Oakley Plantations, regularly scheduled living history re-enactments and hands-on demonstrations keep alive many of the historic skills, lost arts and early plantation practices, and others are revived each spring at the Audubon Pilgrimage's Rural Homestead sponsored by the local historical society, which has played such an important role in preserving and appreciating the past. The St. Francisville area plantations open for daily tours are The Cottage, The Myrtles, Butler Greenwood Plantation, Rosedown, Oakley and Greenwood Plantation.

Oakley Plantation

Completed in the early 1800's, Oakley is decidedly atypical, showing West Indies influence with two full stories and an attic atop a raised basement of brick, its jalousied galleries on both top floors connected by exterior staircases.

Oakley's lands were granted to Ruffin Gray, whose widow married James Pirrie, and it was their beautiful daughter Eliza whose need of a tutor brought the flamboyant artist-naturalist John James Audubon to the plantation in 1821. He was to receive $60 per month plus room and board in exchange for instructing 15-year-old Eliza in dancing, music, drawing, math and French; he was allowed his afternoons free to roam the woods, sketching and collecting specimens, painting a large number of his famous bird studies and cutting quite a dashing figure with his long flowing locks, frilly shirts and satin breeches. Audubon's long-suffering wife Lucy spent several years in the 1820's tutoring neighborhood children at the Robert Percy and William Garrett Johnson plantations, Beech Woods and Beech Grove; when Audubon joined her periodically, he gave the students dancing lessons in the ginhouse and swimming lessons in a deep pool in Big Bayou Sara.

The Cottage Plantation

The land grant is dated 1795

The Cottage's long, rambling main house began as a simple structure of virgin cypress, expanded so skillfully over the years that the front gallery eventually had four French doors and nine windows opening on to it. The house is surrounded by one of the area's most complete plantation complexes of original dependencies, including the outside kitchen and laundry room, commissary, milk house, smokehouse, carriage house containing an 1820 state carriage, several tenant houses and the law office of Judge Thomas Butler, US Congressman and first judge of the area when it became part of the United States in 1810. General Andrew Jackson slept there on his way home from the Battle of New Orleans, since a large contingent of Judge Butler's brothers comprised his most trusted staff.

When David Bradford, Pennsylvania judge and wealthy businessman, obtained the land grant for The Myrtles, he was a fugitive from justice because of his role as leader of the Whiskey Rebellion protesting a tax levied on spirits and other governmental abuses. The small portion of the house Bradford built was purchased and expanded by Judge Clark Woodruff, whose enthusiasm waned upon the untimely deaths of his wife and small daughters in a yellow fever epidemic, and by 1834 The Myrtles had been sold to Ruffin Gray Stirling, who commenced an extensive remodeling which enlarged and formalized the home. A Reconstruction-era murder on the front gallery has given rise to chilling tales of unquiet spirits, and the weekend "ghost tours" are immensely popular.

The Myrtles - 1796

41

Butler Greenwood

...another early raised, rambling English-style cottage on lands granted in the 1790's to Samuel Flower, earliest physician in the area, whose daughter would marry the Chief Justice of the first Louisiana Supreme Court. The house contains the area's finest original formal Victorian parlor, its twelve-piece set of carved rosewood furniture still in the original upholstery, complemented by floor-to-ceiling gilded pier mirrors, floral Brussels carpet, Sevres vases and half a dozen family portraits.

Butler Greenwood is still owned and occupied by the original family, and its lawns and 19th-century gardens are shaded by a huge grove of 200-year-old live oaks and more than 150 tree-sized camellias.

Rosedown

By the time the second and third generations of these plantation families built homes in English Louisiana in the 1830's, they had prospered sufficiently to afford grand Greek Revival structures then in vogue, much more formal and elaborate than the first-generation houses. Rosedown Plantation remains an outstanding example. Built in 1835 by wealthy cotton planter Daniel Turnbull, the lavish double-galleried house is approached by a magnificent oak alley and surrounded by 28 acres of formal gardens designed by Martha Barrow Turnbull, perhaps with the help of a French landscape architect, to equal the grandeur of

Versailles and other great continental gardens she'd seen on her honeymoon. Mrs. Turnbull was without doubt one of the great early southern horticulturists, and her gardening records proved invaluable in the restoration of the grounds, the formal plantings, and the 13 original historic outbuildings.

Greenwood Plantation

Resurrected From The Ashes

Another of the great Greek Revival plantation homes in the St. Francisville area was Greenwood, built in 1830 by William R. Barrow and designed by noted architect James Hammon Coulter. Nearly 100 feet square, the home was surrounded by brick Doric columns, its copper roof topped by a belvedere from which Barrow could survey his lands and look out to the Mississippi. From the time it was opened to the public in the early 1900's by the Frank Percy family, Greenwood was toured by thousands and beloved by Hollywood as a superb setting for movies. During a storm on August 1, 1960, lightning struck the house, and within three hours nothing was left but 28 columns and a few forlorn chimneys. This was enough to touch the heart of one determined family which purchased the site and set about a 15-year reconstruction project to rebuild the home and re-open it to the public as well as the movie industry.

Tilling the Soil

In 1831 the Encyclopaedia Americana called the District of Nueva Feliciana the garden of Louisiana, and always it was so. The verdant hills and well-watered forests, the wonderful wealth of wildflowers...Mother Nature spared no effort in planting this garden spot long before the first settlers arrived.

The first cultivated gardens, quite naturally, were functional ones, the kitchen gardens and truck patches providing vegetables and herbs for cooking and preserving; many of the herbs had medical uses, in addition to seasoning. On the plantations, the vegetable gardens were extensive, providing much of the food consumed by the multi-generational families in the big houses and the ones in the quarters as well. There were pits and cold frames and greenhouses to extend growing seasons and permit the cultivation of exotic tropical plants even during the winter months. To the rear of the main houses stretched the agricultural fields, where slaves and then sharecroppers plowed with mules and weeded with hoes as they tended the cash crops, the indigo and then cotton, some sugar cane, and the large acreage planted in corn that was dried, ground into meal for the family, and fed to the livestock and poultry as well.

As the families prospered, attention could turn from the pragmatic to the merely pleasing. Lawns were cleared, terraced and landscaped, taking full advantage of the natural rolling terrain. Already the cleared grassy grounds brightened early each spring with myriad purple violets and verbena, trillium and other wildflowers, and from the surrounding woodlands were transplanted snowy dogwood and redbud trees, wild oak-leaf hydrangea and lots of shade-loving ferns. Catalogues were ordered from fledgling nurseries on the East Coast, and exotic plants were imported to see which ones could stand the hot southern clime.

ormal gardens were laid out in orderly bordered beds and patterned parterres, protected from roaming livestock by picket fences and presided over by classical marble statues imported from Italy. The gardens were filled with climbing roses and azaleas for bursts of color, hip gardenias and sweet olives to perfume the air; clematis and wisteria vines soon clambered over arches and arbors. Garden paths were bricked and lined with English boxwood, immense cast-iron sugar kettles were filled with water to hold flowering water lilies, peacocks and larger ornamental fowl prowled the grounds while smaller sweet-throated birds serenaded from open-air aviaries. The passing of pleasant hours in these gardens was told by the sun's shadow traversing elaborate sundials.

Great entrance allees were lined with the live oaks that would eventually arch completely across the roadway, their spreading canopies providing all-important shade as well as beauty upon maturity, their branches hung with the Spanish moss so symbolic of southern ambience. Sometimes the avenues led straight to the manors; sometimes they took a meandering path with pleasing curves and teasing vistas, and a rare few were elliptical. On the early places the live oaks were planted in great groves, in the English manner, and the sturdy trees would live for hundreds of years, but the oaks did not rush to maturity. They were far-sighted, these early settlers: you don't plant a live oak for your own generation.

Beginning in the 1830's and 1840's as the great cotton mansions were being built and their grounds landscaped, gardening became the passion of plantation mistresses. This passion was inspired by travels abroad to admire the great gardens of the French chateaux and English castles, and around St. Francisville this passion was happily combined with a fortuitous climate, rich river bottom land soil, unlimited labor and the funds to indulge every whim. A number of magnificent 19th-century gardens pay tribute even today to this early appreciation of the beauties of Nature as enhanced by the hand of man.

Rosedown Plantation, of course, heads the list with its 28 acres of formal gardens conceived by 18-year-old bride Martha Barrow Turnbull on her 1835 wedding trip to the Continent. Only such expansive yet orderly grandeur as she witnessed at Versailles and the other great gardens of Europe could adequately complement the fine plantation home she and her new husband were building. In her gardening diary which spans 60 years, Martha Turnbull recorded the development and expansion of her formal gardens flanking the oak alley leading to the Rosedown house. Her concise records are a testament to the importance of plantings in early southern life and the amazing variety of not just ornamental but also edible plants she set out in her gardens...eggplant and tomatoes, turnips, cabbage, celery, broccoli, beets and spinach, parsnips, carrots, kale, leeks, potatoes, garlic, onions planted at the full moon, peas, dewberries and raspberries, beans, watermelons, cucumbers and cantaloupe, cauliflower, squash, rhutabaga, figs and pears and apples, quince and peaches, plums, artichokes, pineapples in the greenhouse, tobacco and rice.

Mrs. Turnbull was also a very exact diarist, recording her successes and her failures in planting, fertilizing, propagating, rooting cuttings, and beautifying her surroundings, neglecting no detail, even the planting of vines around the ladies' privy. She included astute gardening advice in her diaries, as well as the daily labor. "July 4, 1853: The first rain for six weeks; put down layers of many greenhouse plants and put down tomato slips. Lettuce seed, arbor beans, snaps, watermelons, cauliflower, seed cabbage and celery set out and put down seed, carrots, parsnips, salsify, corn and all sewed. My garden looked deplorable. My violets I planted were gone. But everything now revived... We had on the creek orchard many peach trees, 8 blue figs, 2 pear trees, 11 apples, 9 quinces, 30 azaleas, 13 heliotrope, 15 red flowers from east."

"November 21, 1853: I am now putting down more rose cuttings. Some Japonicas took root...Japonicas must have water over the leaves once a week and plenty of water otherwise during the whole summer; half sand and woods-earth and a little cow manure for the posts when first potted, always in each, and engraft early in the spring, and they must be well shaded in the whole summer. When they are in bloom they require more water and heat than at any other time...It is good to keep the ground around them covered with leaves to keep in the moisture."

One of the first to import camellias

Martha Turnbull was among the first in the South in the 1830's to import camellias, those ornamental natives of the Far East that were initially carried to other lands by missionaries and early medical men after trade with the Orient was opened in the early 1500's by the Portuguese and their Black Ships. The trading companies dealing in spices, silks, porcelains and other treasures all had medical officers who became the first to study native plants of the Far East, initially for their medical propensities, then introduced the botanical oddities back home. A camellia japonica specimen collected in China in 1677 by a physician with the East India Company introduced the plant to England, and toward the close of the 18th century the first camellias were brought to the United States. It was from a nursery in New York that Rosedown first ordered camellias, and soon Martha was setting out hundreds to thrive in the southern climate, along with azaleas, hydrangeas and gardenias.

Rosedown Gardens

Civil War

Destruction and Despair

After the Civil War, the gardening diaries from Rosedown reflect the reduction in the labor force and funds. They are a mixture of despair ("August, 1867: The garden one mass of weeds" and "August, 1872: Cleaned up my yard entirely by my own hands and now hawling manure and trash from Eliza's side") and a gardener's delight in the renewed promises of springtime ("1874: The violet bed is very pretty") and the acceptance that the work is never done ("April, 1891: A shower just to lay the dust; pinched off all chrysanthemums to blooms; chickens disturb my roses terrible").

Very Little Help

The war years brought horrific hardships and adjustment to a new way of life on the plantations. Before the Civil War there were some 450 slaves on Rosedown, but one wartime recording laments that 129 of them were "with the Yankees," a few with the Confederates or other relatives and nearly 40 dead, leaving 178 on the plantation, some clearly not thrilled to have been left behind. The 1869 diary recordings mention one servant, ordered to scrub the kitchen, who "walked off and sat in her house for 3 days," and another "was impudent and would not cook, Elry laid up regularly every 12 days for 9 days, Lucinda refused to come and wait on me, Virg got sick when sent for to come up here to work." But still the gardening work went on. Martha Turnbull was replaced by her daughter Sarah, who married James Pirrie Bowman, son of Oakley's Eliza Pirrie and the rector of Grace Church. They had ten children, eight of them girls...Miss Martha, Miss Eliza, Miss Sarah, Miss Anna, Miss Mamie, Miss Nina, Miss Corrie and Miss Belle, a number of whom remained at Rosedown all their lives, unmarried, struggling in their turn to keep up the gardens and home.

Catalpa Plantation
Home of William J. Fort

Always Martha Turnbull heeded advice from neighbors, including the Forts of Catalpa Plantation (handsome William J. Fort was so taken with the beautiful Bowman sisters that he would marry not one but two of Martha's granddaughters). Writes Mrs. Turnbull in her diary, "Mrs. Fort puts one gallon Guano to a barrel of water to water her plants once a week to make them grow, and to her green house plants 1/2 gallon Guano 1/2 gallon Ashes to a barrel of water and then to a pint of the mixture put a pint of clear water and water once a week." It was no wonder, then, that the three-story greenhouse at the Fort plantation was such a wonder, in which flourished exotics like cinnamon, guava, mandarins, tropical plants, tea and coffee, bananas and orange trees, plus flowering potted plants and vines.

"There is always such a good time to be had at the Forts," the saying went a century or more ago, with the lawns laid out for pleasure, wisteria-draped summer houses and a pavilion for dancing, a fish pond centered by a fountain and an island for fishfries and picnics, a deer park, flocks of preening peacocks and swans, and the rare elliptical oak avenue lined with enormous pink conch shells in such quantities that there was one servant whose sole occupation was keeping them polished.

By the 1840's the formal and sunken gardens at Butler Greenwood Plantation were being developed by Harriett Flower Mathews, and dozens of camellias in many hues were imported for the landscaping there as well. Amid the boxwood parterres to the north of the 1790's plantation house, camellia japonicas shipped from "Up East" were planted to complement the

lovely lattice-sided Victorian summer house, still shaded by an immense ancient gingko tree whose leaves turn brilliant yellow in the fall. Sweet olives and magnolia fuscata scrubs planted by Harriett in the mid-1800's today tower 20 to 30 feet high, and the camellias, sasanquas and tea trees are now tree-sized as well. A dozen cast-iron urns grace brick pedestals across the

grounds, along with lacy iron benches. These gardens were among only a few dozen in the nation considered significant enough to be recorded by the Historic American Buildings Survey in the thirties. As at Oakley Plantation and other antebellum landscapes, there are literally hundreds and hundreds of old-fashioned ardesias, their scarlet berries enlivening the winter landscape even today, every berry that hits the ground sprouting in the rich woods-earth.

Beauty among the Ruins

Another magnificent antebellum garden which is open seasonally in the St. Francisville area is Afton Villa, where the impressive oak alley underplanted with Pride of Afton azaleas and the surrounding landscaping are all that remain on the site of a flamboyant mansion built in the 1850's and burned in the 1960's.

Recent owners have turned what could have been a heart-breaking site into a garden spot of breathtaking beauty. Flowering vines clamber across the crumbling brick ruins, and masses of bulbs---thousands and thousands of jonquils, daffodils, narcissus, tulips and others brighten the terraced lawns in early spring.

Formal parterres are set off with ancient camellias, and here, as at the other antebellum gardens, there seems to be a happy marriage between the japonicas and the moss-draped live oaks providing just the right amount of filtered sunlight and shade for a perfection of performance. A small family cemetery contains a monument erected by Congress upon the death in 1846 of Senator Alexander Barrow, called the handsomest man in Washington.

IN MEMORY OF
ALEXANDER BARROW
BORN IN THE STATE
OF
TENNESSEE,
MARCH 27TH 1801.
DIED IN BALTIMORE,
DEC'R. 29TH 1846.
BEING AT THE TIME A SENATOR IN
CONGRESS FROM THE STATE OF
LOUISIANA, OF WHICH HE HAD BEEN
A CITIZEN FOR TWENTY-FIVE YEARS

In the historic little 19th-century rivertown of St. Francisville, where the entire downtown area is listed on the National Register of Historic Places, there's not a single Victorian house without its prized camellia blooming through the winter, masses of azaleas in the spring, climbing roses clambering over trellises and brightly hued daylilies poking through picket fences on hot sultry summer days. And then there are the colorful crape myrtle trees, their masses of bloom the staple of the southern summer garden, almost as plentiful as the live oaks; nearly every town lawnscape has some, in watermelon pink or lavender, in red or white. Fortuitously for visitors, these private town gardens are easily enjoyed on walking or driving tours, and local gardening groups have landscaped small pocket gardens as resting spots for strollers.

Every historic home in the St. Francisville area had its glorious garden, thoughtfully planned so that there was always a pleasant fragrance in the air and colorful blooms nearly every season of the year; some remain, and some are but a memory. The flowering bulbs and

periwinkle and phlox struggle up through unkempt lawns to mark former house sites, and sometimes the sturdy climbing roses, as Miss Louise Butler observed, are left "upholding a summer house in ruins or the rotting timbers of an arbor so sequestered as to have heard, doubtless, the love vows of four or five generations, while on the lips that breathed them, time has laid a silencing finger." And the majestic live oaks long outlive their planter, giving shade and shelter to succeeding generations, just as he must have hoped.

59

Marble statues guard the ruins of beautiful Afton Villa gardens

Praising

the

Lord

Sowing the Gospel

The land was cleared, the homes were built and the crops laid in. It was time to praise the Lord from whom all blessings flowed. But frontier religious worship was tenuous at best. There were itinerant preachers who sowed the gospel like seeds, scattering a handful of sermons and then moving on, not able to stick around to see if the seeds bore fruit. There were fiery missionaries like Lorenzo Dow, who blazed a trail through the area and lit a fire in hearts and souls. Congregants came together where they could, meeting in private homes or public places. The earliest organized congregation of black slaves met in a hollow in the deep woods, while the Jewish congregation met in Bayou Sara in a hotel and then an opera house before they could construct their Temple Sinai in St. Francisville, and the early Roman Catholics held services on the upper floor of the old Bayou Sara market house until it was burned by the Yankees and then in homes or the courthouse until the present church was built.

The oldest church in St. Francisville,

hauntingly beautiful Grace Episcopal Church, was established in 1827 as the second oldest Episcopal congregation in the state, with Thomas Butler and William Flower as wardens and a vestry

composed of Ira Smith, Edward H. Barton, Henry Flower, Francis Dabney, Robert Young, Louis Stirling, John Mulholland, Benjamin House, Levi Blunt and John L. Lobdell. Called to serve as first rector was the Reverend William R. Bowman, who became the second husband of widowed Eliza Pirrie of Oakley Plantation, and their son married the beautiful belle Sarah Turnbull of Rosedown. In the parochial report to the annual convention in 1838, Grace Church reported 14 white and 31 colored infant baptisms for the year, 7 white and 25 colored adult baptisms, three marriages and 14 funerals; by 1845 there were 26 communicants, and in 1849 the rector's salary was a lordly $1002 a year.

The present church,

second on the same spot, is a picturesque brick structure reminiscent of the Gothic country churches that dot the English countryside. Its cornerstone was laid in June, 1858 by Leonidas Polk, Bishop of Louisiana who headed the state diocese and later served as a major general during the Civil War. Known as the Fighting Bishop of

the Confederacy, he would be killed at the Battle of Pine Mountain in 1864. Exceptional early American stained glass windows filter the sunlight across carved faux-bois oak pews, some of which have been occupied by members of the same families for generations. The immense Pilcher organ built into the south transcept was shipped downriver from St. Louis in 1858 as a memorial to Judge George Mathews of Butler Greenwood Plantation and is the oldest two-manual tracker-action organ still in use in the country; playing it is not for the faint-hearted nor the feeble, and at one point it had to be manu-

ally pumped by the sexton, who often fell asleep at the post, causing the organist to have to dismount from her bench to arouse him.

The cemetery at Grace Church

The peaceful oak-shaded cemetery is filled with fine statuary and Victorian monuments of marble and stone, some with ornately carved pillars, Grecian drapery, elaborate floral carvings and flowing epitaphs. Among the earliest of burials in the 1840's was that of baby Edward Baldwin, whose cause of death, no doubt a common one in those days of runaway horses and rutted roads and open carriages, was recorded as "flung from buggy."

The shelling of St. Francisville

During the Civil War, St. Francisville was shelled by the USS Lafayette for four long hours on January 16, 1864, and the church, its bell tower all too visible above the treeline from the river, was severely damaged. Old Aunt Silvia Chew, free

woman of color in the neighborhood, took refuge before the altar until a cannon ball whizzed over her head and crashed through the window; she then fled to the cemetery and put her faith in the substantially built tomb of her old acquaintance Dr. Ira Smith, surviving to tell the tale and to later sell to Grace Church several lots of property to expand the cemetery.

Another of St. Francisville's beautiful historic churches is Our Lady of Mount Carmel Catholic Church, perched high on a bluff overlooking the Mississippi River. It was completed in 1893 from plans drawn by Civil War hero General P.G.T. Beauregard.

On nearby Royal St. in the midst of St. Francisville's historic district is the lovely little United Methodist Church, built in 1899 with splendid simplicity of style, replacing an earlier church in Bayou Sara that had galleries wide enough to accommodate dozens of slaves during services and also large numbers of townsfolk seeking high ground during recurrent spring floods.

Religion among the black population

There are now dozens of small predominately black Baptist churches scattered around the St. Francisville area, but before the Civil War plantation owners of the Felicianas attempted to provide for

the spiritual life of their slaves primarily by involving them in their own systems of belief. With the Civil War, however, came a reluctance of blacks to be dominated by former masters in matters of religion, as well as a groundswell of interest in the new black Baptist movement. A congregation of several hundred freed slaves had been meeting at Clover Hill Plantation, gathering twice a month in the woods in a hollow between two steep banks. In 1871 the congregation found a more desirable home.

Compassionate Susan Barrow

To please his new wife Susan, in 1849 David Barrow began construction of a flamboyant forty-room French Gothic-Victorian chateau on Afton Villa Plantation, and when she moved from her Kentucky home, Susan brought with her a slave named Jenny Lind, no doubt for the celebrated Swedish songstress who toured the country in the 1850's under the management of P.T. Barnum. Raised by Mrs. Barrow, Jenny Lind was considered one of the family, and when she married George Tilly on New Year's Day 1867, the ceremony was performed in the formal parlor at Afton Villa. Both Jenny and George could read and write, but many of their contemporaries could not. This so concerned compassionate Susan Barrow that, with her husband's support, she donated to the Afton Villa Colored Baptist Church a small piece of land valued at $50 for the purpose of erecting a church and school. Former members of the Clover Hill congregation raised a single-room frame church built by some of the founders, men skilled with a hammer and saw who could neither read nor write and who signed the church documents with an X.

The Afton Villa Church
Still making a joyful sound to the Lord

The Afton Villa Church has had only ten pastors in its century-plus years of service, including George Tilly and the Reverend Sam Johnson who served the Lord there for nearly half a century until his recent retirement. This stability of guidance, combined with the fact that many congregation members are descendants of the founding families, surely has helped to preserve many of the traditional practices of worship at Afton Villa Church, for while material improvements have been effected over the years, the services and celebrations remain for the most part unchanged, and when the choir marches in making joyful music unto the Lord, the centuries blur in the timelessness of worship.

Adding to the roll

Baptizing is in late summer. "Some years," according to longtime church member Violet Pate, "we have good baptizing, 30 to 40 head; other years nobody wants to get religion." Candidates are now washed of their sins in a pool behind the church, but until recently the baptizings were held at

nearby plantation ponds, where white-clad candidates were liberally immersed and cleansed of sin. Wake services are held at the church the night before burial. In the old days the body was transported to the church in a huge, black glass-windowed covered wagon pulled by mules, and wakes lasted throughout the night. "The old folks," Violet Pate recalls, "always sat up all night with the dead; they said it was the last they could do for them, to wake them right." Funeral services are marked by music, eulogies, obituaries and condolences. If the deceased held church office, it is customary to "veil" his usual seat and leave it vacant for 30 days out of respect. In the peaceful oak-shaded cemetery, some headstones are rustic concrete ones scratched with simple names and decoration.

A time for celebration

Each year the Afton Villa Church anniversary is celebrated with the theme from Psalms: "We have heard with our ears and our forefathers have told us what work Thou didest in the days of old." Violet Pate says the theme is apt. "The old-timers really have told us about the old days, how they used to walk to church with lanterns at night, and how they'd walk barefooted along the dirt roads and clean their feet with a rag before putting on their shoes to enter the church."

Where other religious communities are only now reviving an interest in history and heritage, Afton Villa Baptist Church never lost its awareness of its beginnings or its appreciation for those who went before, and neither did Grace Episcopal or United Methodist or Our Lady of Mount Carmel Churches. All of these still hold services at which visitors are welcome, and there are also historic cemeteries to visit in the area, in addition to those around existing

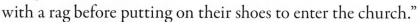

church structures. Most notable is Locust Grove Cemetery, now a State Historic Site, the final resting place of Sarah Knox Taylor Davis, first wife of Confederate President Jefferson Davis and daughter of U.S. President Zachary Taylor; she succumbed to yellow fever as a young bride while visiting relatives on Davis' sister's plantation. Another grave at Locust Grove is that of little Aurelia Ripley, born and died in the 1830's, whose epitaph reads: "Stranger, If E'er these Lines Be Read, Weep For The Living, Not The Dead."

Celebrations of
the Seasons

In the northeast the arrival of fall is heralded by brilliantly colored foliage, and St. Francisville too can enjoy orange-red swamp maples and sumac and the golden yellow of ginko trees after the first few frosts, though not nearly to the same extent. And you know it's spring in St. Francisville when the fruit trees and Japanese magnolias flower and the azaleas bloom, and it has to be summertime when the crepe myrtles and roses brighten the gardens, or the camellias in the winter.

But St. Francisville really marks the passing of the seasons by its special events, in themselves celebrations of the seasons more colorful than any curly maple. If you see locals dressed in the garb of the 1820's when the artist Audubon resided among them, it's sure to be The Audubon

Pilgrimage time in the spring. If you see elaborate antebellum dresses and Civil War uniforms, both Yankee blue and Confederate grey, you know it's summertime and the commemoration of The Day The War

Stopped. Fall finds everybody decked out in cowboy gear heading toward the Wildest Show in the South, the prison rodeo at Angola. And wintertime, well, of course that's when Santa visits; sometimes he arrives in a decorated wagon pulled by prancing draft horses with brass harness bells jingling, and sometimes he's atop the town fire engine or even the bright red Coca-Cola truck, but he always manages to make it in time for the lighting of the town Christmas tree and the ensuing celebration of the season that make St. Francisville's Christmas in the Country a well-loved alternative to mall madness.

The Audubon Pilgrimage

for more than three decades has celebrated the well-preserved history of one of Louisiana's unique cultural corners, set against a backdrop of the splendors of a southern spring. Always the third weekend each March when the azaleas are at their peak of bloom, the tour welcomes spring by opening the doors to historic mansions and gardens not normally accessible to visitors, with elegantly costumed hostesses and demonstrations of rustic old-time skills. Proceeds benefit historic preservation and an enhanced understanding of the past for both visitors and residents alike. It's all done in tribute to the artist Audubon and the impact his tenure had on the area...and vice versa.

Audubon...The world's most famous wildlife artist

Having set for himself the staggering task of painting all of the birds of this immense fledgling country, John James Audubon arrived in St. Francisville by steamboat in 1821, penniless and with a string of failed business ventures behind him, but rich in talent and dreams. Hired to tutor the beautiful young daughter of Oakley Plantation, he was allowed his afternoons free to roam the woods, sketching and collecting specimens, and he would paint a large number of his famous bird folios in this area.

Born in 1785 in Santa Domingo, Audubon was the son of a French ship captain and his Creole mistress. He was reared in France and then sent to America in 1803, still in his teens but already exhibiting a decided artistic bent, to learn English and a trade on his father's Pennsylvania estate. By 1812, the year Louisiana became a state, the young artist had married and fathered two sons, but he chafed under the bonds of practical employment,

longing instead to be at his nature studies in the woods. In 1820 he set out for New Orleans with only his gun, flute, violin, bird books, portfolios of his own drawings, chalks, watercolors, drawing papers in a tin box, and a dog-eared journal. He earned a meager living painting portraits and giving lessons in drawing, dancing and more scholastic subjects, but by the following year Audubon was established at Oakley Plantation near St. Francisville and well on his way to accomplishing his amazing task.

Historic homes such as Oakley, Rosedown and Afton Villa are featured on the pilgrimage as are others carefully chosen to provide a glimpse of life as it was in 19th-century St. Francisville. Hostess costumes authentically re-create the resplendent gowns of the 1820's, the period during which Audubon was in residence at Oakley, and the Audubon Pilgrimage has won national recognition for its astute attention to historical detail, both in its costuming and in its thoroughly professional and interesting interpretive tours.

In addition to the tours, there are special activities throughout St. Francisville during the pilgrimage. Exuberant costumed children dance the Maypole and play nostalgic games during the day, and old-fashioned hymn singing at the United Methodist Church enlivens the night. The Rural Homestead, with its simple structures of hand-hewn cypress shingles and ancient timbers, shows how most ordinary folk lived in the 19th century, with demonstrations of the old-time skills necessary for survival...wood-stove and open-hearth cooking, basket weaving, quilting, carding and spinning, grinding cornmeal with a gristmill, riving shingles by hand with a froe, plowing with a mule; add lively bluegrass music in the background and you've got the makings for a real old-fashioned spring frolic.

Following hot on the heels of the Audubon Pilgrimage is another event the artist-naturalist would have enjoyed, the Audubon Country Birdfest showcasing the huge population of birds, both resident and migratory, the area harbored in Audubon's day and continues to harbor today. Guided field trips transport birders into unique habitat areas in some of the remote reaches of the parish, and there

are lectures, vendors and beginning birder sessions as well. This is usually the first weekend in April, and later in the summer the Hummingbird Festival highlights observation and banding of those brightly colored tiny feathered friends, both festivals inherently suited for this unspoiled region called Audubon Country.

Fall in the Felicianas heralds the area's liveliest activity, the annual Angola Prison Rodeo, the "Wildest Show in the South," at Louisiana State Penitentiary just north of St. Francisville. Prison bands entertain and incarcerated craftsmen sell all manner of artwork, but the real highlight is the rodeo, begun in 1964 solely as entertainment for correctional officers and a few foolhardy inmate cowboys, now grown into one of the area's most popular events. From the time the mounted black-shirted Angola Rough Riders charge into the 10,000-seat covered arena at full gallop with flags flying, the spectators are on the edges of their seats as they watch inmates compete in regular professional rodeo events like bareback bronc riding, bulldogging and bull riding.

"The Wildest Show in the South

"The Day The War Stopped"

Jump forward four decades from the time of Audubon's stay in the area. In June of 1863, the Civil War siege of Port Hudson was pitting 30,000 Union troops under Major General Nathaniel P. Banks against 6,800 weary Confederates under Major General Franklin Gardner, fighting over the all-important control of traffic on the Mississippi, Port Hudson and Vicksburg being the only rebel strongholds left along the river. Only two federal gunboats made it through the blockade at Port Hudson to St. Francisville, one the USS Albatross, the other Admiral David Farragut's flagship. Grace Church became the focus of one of the most touching moments of civility during this long and bloody battle, when the war stopped long enough to permit the burial in Grace's cemetery of the Albatross' commander.

Lt. Commander John E. Hart of New York,

having "suicided" most probably in the delirium of malaria, was a Mason; W.W. Leake, Confederate defender of St. Francisville, was senior warden of the Feliciana Lodge No. 31, F&AM, in St. Francisville and was in the area, "his headquarters being in the saddle." As a soldier, Leake said, it was his duty to permit the burial of deceased members of the armed forces of any government, and as a Mason it was his duty to accord Masonic burial to the remains of a brother Mason regardless of circumstances in the outside world. And so during a brief ceasefire this Yankee Mason

was laid to rest in the cemetery his gunboat had been shelling, accorded the dignity in death of rites conducted by both Confederate and Union brother Masons as well as the Episcopal rector. "The Day The War Stopped" is re-created every year in June, with parades, drama, re-enactment of the burial, vintage music and period dancing.

Everybody's favorite small town Christmas celebration

Millions of tiny white lights trace soaring Victorian trimwork and grace gallery posts to transform this quaint little nineteenth-century rivertown into a veritable winter wonderland as it celebrates Christmas in the Country, always the first full weekend in December. But the splendid decorations last throughout the month, joined by spectacular natural displays of blossoming camellias all over town and in the nearby antebellum plantation gardens.

Strolling musical groups and bands join the angelic voices of children's choirs, bell-ringers and dancers, food vendors and crafts, a living nativity scene, Christmas carols, children's breakfast with Santa, face-painting and all manner of entertainment; even the resident dogs join the fun sporting Santa hats.

The Historical District of St. Francisville, thanks to an enthusiastic Main Street Program and sensitive preservation regulations, maintains its historic character hand-in-hand with present day economic viability. This downtown area is very much alive, in fact the center of life in the community; a variety of quaint little shops occupy historic structures throughout the area, each unique in its own way, and visitors should not miss a single one.

The real focal point of Christmas in the country remains the St. Francisville area's marvelous little shops, and they go all out for this special weekend, hosting Open Houses with refreshments and entertainment for shoppers while offering spectacular seasonal decorations and great gift items. The merchants of St. Francisville started Christmas in the Country several decades ago as a way to entice residents and visitors downtown to do their Christmas shopping, and the event has been a much-loved herald of the season ever since.

Merry Christmas

The Christmas Parade
Sponsored by the Women's Service League

Today, The Past is Present

Mamie Fort Thompson
Grande dame of the Felicianas

Descendant of Eliza Pirrie of Oakley Plantation and the Forts of Catalpa and the Turnbulls of Rosedown, Miss Mamie conducted paying guests through her beloved home, Catalpa Plantation, well into her 90's and shared a glass or two (or maybe three) of sherry with every single one of them. A lifelong flirt and fun-loving tease with a delicious wit, she'd tell tourists about the cast-iron greyhounds guarding the entrance; if the visitors were northern, she'd point out the bullet hole put there by a plain old Yankee soldier during the Civil War, but for southern visitors, it was a "damn Yankee."

When she coyly showed off the charming portrait of her grandmother Sarah Turnbull, the "National Belle" of 1849, and mentioned that the beauteous Sarah had received 100 proposals, courtly gentlemen callers couldn't help but respond, "If I'd been alive then, she'd have had 101!" Miss Mamie introduced visitors from around the world to a startling concept long known by southern gentlemen: old Southern Belles never die, nor do they lose one iota of their charm, which is only sharpened and enhanced by the patina and lustre of passing time.

Pat and Laurie Walsh

The St. Francisville area abounds in wonderful Bed & Breakfasts, from lakeside clubhouses to restored plantations, from golf resorts to historic townhouses. One of the most popular is the St. Francisville Inn right in the heart of the historic district, a European-type country inn complete with landscaped bricked courtyard, bountiful breakfast buffet and evening wine bar. Proprietors are Pat and Laurie Walsh. She serves as the town's Main Street director, and he is the local computer whiz building fabulous web sites for every entity in the area when he's not birdwatching from his kayak in remote reaches of Cat Island swamp; together they are involved in every local activity and event.

Reverend Samuel Johnson

For half a century, kindly Rev. Samuel Marshall Johnson shepherded the flock at Afton Villa Baptist Church, the oldest black church in the St. Francisville area, dating from 1871. Age 94 when photographed, he has retired from both Afton Villa and St. Peter, which he also served for 47 years, but he rarely misses a Sunday in attendance at one or the other of several churches he pastored over the years.

Joe Savell

Bearded Joe Savell took a little detour between his college studies in Visual Design and running his own Backwoods Art Gallery in St. Francisville when he served for 18 years as the rural route mail deliveryman in areas so isolated he often found snakes and other wildlife in the mail boxes. Now his gallery exhibits his own and other artists' works, but he still makes special deliveries in his own special way: walking to work every morning just as downtown St. Francisville is waking up, he thoughtfully takes time to put elderly residents' newspapers up on their porches.

Elisabeth Kilbourne Dart

Researcher and writer, historian and musician, equestrian and swimmer, Libby Dart is, quite simply, St. Francisville's historical conscience, encouraging the preservation of significant structures and insisting upon a properly authentic appreciation of the past. She regularly contributes thoughtful articles to historic journals and magazines as well as the local newspaper, has compiled an impressive research catalog on every aspect of local life from the most minute detail to the broad overview, and spearheaded the Audubon Pilgrimage at which for years she appeared on her own horse in 19th-century ladies' riding habit complete with vintage sidesaddle. As longtime head of the West Feliciana Historical Society, she commanded the entire community to get involved in preservation and the pilgrimage, and she made sure they did it, by God, with a smile! Ever since she was a five-year-old piano student she has wrestled with the huge

Pilcher organ in Grace Episcopal Church to provide music for some Sunday services as well as the funerals of several generations of parishioners, playing, as she puts it, "poorly but devoutly."

Emily Smothers

Nothing brightens the wait at the landing for the ferry that crosses the Mississippi River from St. Francisville to New Roads like the sight of "Miss Emily" Smothers with her bright red wagon loaded with homemade pralines and boiled or roasted peanuts. With her trusty walking stick and straw hat, Miss Emily has been braving the breezes and broiling sun to peddle her pralines along the river for several decades. These days, she just goes when she feels up to it, and sometimes she lets a grandson take her place.

Lloyd L. Lindsey, Jr.

Career educator descended from several of Louisiana's State Superintendents of Education, Lloyd Lindsey is currently the parish superintendent of schools and has turned a moribund educational system into one of the best public school systems in the state. But he's also an avid organic gardener and farmer (his vegetable garden covers a full acre), raises registered bird dogs and mules (he lets some Amish friends "put a good work ethic in them"), and during the annual Audubon Pilgrimage, he sheds his customary bow-tie, dons overalls and plows a perfectly straight furrow behind his mules Samson and Kate at the Rural Homestead. Lloyd poses in front of the Julius Freyhan School, St. Francisville's first public school facility dating from the early 1900's.

Asarine Cobb

A cast-iron wood stove in the main room keeps Asarine Cobb's tiny hillside home comfortable even in winter, and after a lifetime of farming cotton, potatoes, corn, beans and peanuts, she's content to rest and share the wisdom gained over her 78 years. These young people today, she decries, don't stick with marriage like they should; "you've got to shake it and take it," she advises, and make an effort to work things out. She confesses she did leave her own husband once, and then she came back, but she warned him if she ever had to leave again, she was staying gone, and she meant it. She never had to leave again.

Roland Barber

This career engineer now applies that same precision and attention to detail to the exquisite bird carvings he creates from tupelo wood in his retirement. His offspring are just as creative and have turned a disintegrating corner of downtown St. Francisville into colorful and lively Bohemianville. Daughter Robin developed Magnolia Cafe' from a gas station peddling health food into everybody's favorite downtown restaurant

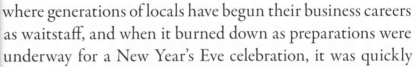

where generations of locals have begun their business careers as waitstaff, and when it burned down as preparations were underway for a New Year's Eve celebration, it was quickly resurrected from the ashes by community demand and has been expanding ever since. Daughter Lynn, a painter and free spirit herself, started the nextdoor Birdman Books and Coffee as an eclectic mix of coffee house/art gallery/book store.

Both are local gathering places where you can see the entire population of St. Francisville in a matter of minutes (the Klein sisters, whose late father was longtime rector at Grace Episcopal, are breakfast regulars), and both host periodic live musical performances, art festivals and all manner of stimulating stuff.

Miss Pinky's Cabin

Pinky Jackson lives in Corner, which consists of not much more than Pinky's house and the historic McCausland Cemetery just up the road toward the Mississippi state line and Westmoreland Plantation where Pinky cooked for the Woods family for years. On a small hill beneath a towering shadetree, Pinky's tidy home is the perfect small house, approached by a winding pathway bordered by neat flowerbeds, and she keeps it so meticulously clean you could eat off the well-swept dirt yard, not to mention the floor. Fishing poles are propped against the chimney, and even the dogs and cats looked contented and well cared for. In front, the face of the house visible to the road is whitewashed, with dark green trim for the shutters and porch swing and gallery rail; the back of the house, however, is a whole different ball game, a hodge-podge of cobbled mismatched weathered boards and pieces of tin and roofing felt to keep the cold winds out.

The Metz Brothers

There were six handsome, rugged Metz brothers and two sisters born into an old logging family of German descent who lived in almost total self-sufficiency near Cat Island along the Mississippi

River. These two were christened Carl and Julius, but are universally known as Dump and Moochie, both now in their 70's but still active and still raising or producing nearly everything they need. Moochie has an extensive cattle operation and Dump, the baby of the family, rives cypress shingles the old-time way with a hand froe, much in demand for restoration roofing. And boy, can they tell some tales!

Louise Williams

The peaceful serenity of her face belies her age. Born on June 15, 1900, Louise Williams has seen a lot of changes in her 107 years. An accomplished seamstress who also worked in the fields and did housework, she had only one child who survived infancy, but now has 6 grandchildren, 10 great-grandchildren and 4 great-great-grandchildren. Still alert and lively, she was baptized in 1917 at St. Paul Baptist Church in Weyanoke, where she is now the Mother of the Church and still reads her Sunday School lessons herself. Mrs. Williams recalls standing on a roadbank to marvel at the first automobile that passed her way (nobody knew what it was). When the first airplane flew overhead, she recalls people hiding under the house until it passed; she swore she'd never ride in one, but took her first and last airplane ride in 1999 all the way to California for her brother's funeral.

Bill & Leona Plettinger

A truly inspiring love story, their marriage has lasted for over 72 happy and busy years; when they were photographed, Mr. Bill was 94 and his wife, 92. She was the third generation of her family to serve as Postmaster of Weyanoke, a small community above St. Francisville in the Tunica Hills. She operated the post office combined with a little country store opened in 1934 in their neat wood-frame home, while he farmed, raised cattle, ran a dairy, ground sassafrass into file to sell in New Orleans, drove a school bus and served for years on the school board.

Willie Monroe

Unfailingly pleasant and smiling, Willie worked construction jobs and at the Tunica Sawmill in the Tunica Hills. He also farmed cotton and sweet potatoes, and until arthritis got the best of him the year he turned 89, he raised a huge and productive vegetable garden to feed his wife Mathilda, daughters, grandchildren and great-grandchildren.

93

Murrell Butler

As a child he admired the Audubons hanging on the walls of his grandparents' plantation home; now his own works hang on those very same walls, and while he modestly demurs at any comparison to Audubon, he has obviously been inspired by many of the same settings and wealth of subject matter in the St. Francisville area. Immensely talented artist Murrell Butler has create a landscaped oasis in the midst of a cow pasture for his rustic log home-studio, surrounded by plantings that attract the birds he has studied and painted his entire life. Here he finds the inspiration for his award-winning works, as well as in the cypress swamps and lush landscapes of his native state.

Hester Eby

With quiet dignity, Director of Tours Hester Eby has conducted visitors through The Myrtles for more than twenty years, maintaining her decorum even while telling lurid tales of all the unquiet spirits said to haunt this historic home. Through the course of many different owners, Hester's steadfast presence provides stability and continuity as this fascinating property is shared with tourists.

Mayor Billy D'Aquilla

Jovial Billy D'Aquilla was elected to the St. Francisville City Council in 1972 and served 12 years, 8 of them as Mayor Pro Temp. In 1984 he ran for mayor and was elected; in the two decades since then, he's been returned to office every four years without opposition. Why? Because Billy D'Aquilla absolutely loves his town and he absolutely loves his job. He has presided over progressive improvements like a new 500,000-gallon water tower, new

fire trucks and sewage system, ball fields, and enhanced tourism promotion. He's most proud of the downtown

development plan, to be implemented in stages, that created a lovely oak-shaded park with bandstand gazebo in the center of downtown, public restrooms and bricked sidewalks, and will culminate in a riverwalk to capitalize on a wasted resource, the town's riverside entrance. And besides all that, as daylight breaks on pilgrimage mornings Billy D'Aquilla is just as likely to be out on the town tractor manicuring the grass, and when parades are over he's right out there with the town workcrew picking up trash. Did we mention he's the perfect mayor?

Rosalee Pate

An outgoing, friendly and caring person with a great sense of humor (and a wicked natural-born mimic), her career was in providing services to the elderly through the Council on Aging and most recently in dispensing hospitality to Bed & Breakfast guests. Her husband Buck was well respected throughout the community as one of the first black deputy sheriffs in rural West Feliciana Parish, a dangerous job in the days when Louisiana's maximum-security prison at Angola, then the bloodiest penitentiary in America and only about 20 miles northwest of St. Francisville, was the scene of plenty of hair-raising escapes.

Lucy Parlange

Married in Grace Episcopal Church, lovely Miss Lucy presides with husband Walter over magnificent 1750 Parlange Plantation, a National Historic Landmark across the Mississippi from St. Francisville, her beauty undiminished by the passing years and ever one of the South's most gracious hostesses. One Parlange ancestor scandalized 1880's society in Paris when painted with provocative stance and daring decolletage in John Singer Sargent's masterpiece portrait of Madame X, but the only thing excessive about the present Mrs. Parlange is her great exuberance for life and her unfailing kindness to friends and strangers alike.

Johnny Harris

At age 80, Johnny Harris meticulously maintains the fifty acres of lawns and formal gardens at Butler Greenwood Plantation on a daily basis, but in his long career he has farmed sweet potatoes, worked construction and on the railroad. He's also a church-going happily married man and the father of 21 children, "16 head of them living." And his 30-year-old doctor says he wishes he were half as healthy.

Brother Harold Babin

When he retired recently from St. Francisville's picturesque United Methodist Church, Brother Babin had served that congregation for 33 long and fruitful years, but his heart was so full of love and compassion and caring that he managed to touch the lives of nearly everybody in the entire community, regardless of denomination. He always loved getting dressed up in vintage vestments to participate in the Audubon Pilgrimage each spring.

John Flippen

Living history demonstrations and re-enactments bring the past vividly to life for present-day visitors. John Flippen, a great lover of history, belongs to both Union and Confederate re-enactment units and has Civil War uniforms for each, authentic down to the worn brogans and belt buckles. He is also a member of the Louisiana Vintage Dancers, recreating elegant balls and camp dances wearing a splendid Regency frock coat complete with tails.

Wayne Zuccarella

While his laid-back approach to life in general may seem easy going, there's certainly nothing casual about Wayne Zuccarella's meticulous approach to woodworking. For 32 years he worked under the demanding eyes of A. Hays Town, dean of Louisiana architects who worked nearly until his death at 101 and required absolute perfection in even the most minute detail. Like his uncle W.A. Coco before him, Wayne did all the specialty hand-carvings, millwork, cabinet work and turned woods for Mr. Town, and there could have been no better teacher. Now Wayne specializes in spectacular staircases, and the beauty of the hand-turned newel posts and spindles in his soaring spiral and circular stairs can take

the breath away. Rosedown Plantation's restoration specialists searched around the world for a craftsman able to turn massive solid cypress replacement posts for its gallery, then found the perfect craftsman right under their noses.

Donna Metz

Donna and her sisters Tracey and Chaille grew up in the old Martin home called Beech Grove, right on the scenic sunken Old Tunica Road, and they loved nothing better than riding horseback through the surrounding unspoiled wilderness areas. Now Donna shares that pleasure by renting gaited horses from her Cross Creek Stables.

The Spirit of St. Francisville

The sheer nerve, the absolute audacity, to think that we could capture the essence of a little community like St. Francisville, resonating with romance, resounding with the echoes of history, influenced by settlers both early and late whose lives and loves and labors drew sustenance from the fertile soil in which they'd put down roots. Understanding and chronicling its character, its culture and its color, its soul and its spirit--a hopeless undertaking, it might seem, to even conceive of conveying the sights and smells and sounds that make this spot so special. And yet, and yet...perhaps through carefully chosen words and the poetic images of an artist in love with the place, a bit of that soul and timeless charm might be preserved in the pages of this book.

There are, after all, so many clues as to what made this particular place so pleasing, so many vestiges of the past around to guide us---the weathered boards of

timeworn buildings, the ancient live oaks, the sunken footpaths and the stern ancestors in oil gazing from parlor walls--glimpses through wavy handblown panes of lace-curtained windows. And the Past, as a wiser wordsmith than I often said, in the South the Past isn't even past. It certainly isn't in St. Francisville.

And so you have the sweating rosy-cheeked cooks of Rosedown Plantation preparing over the outside kitchen's open hearth the very same dishes from the very same recipes as did the Turnbull family who built the place in the 1830's.

You have the same riotous and raucous bird population crowding the ancient treetops of Oakley Plantation that inspired artist John James Audubon in the 1820's. You have the same rustic quarters that once housed slave families tilling the soil of The Cottage Plantation now being used in the filming of a modern movie written by respected black author Ernest Gaines.

You have visitors touring Butler Greenwood Plantation considering which ancestral portrait most closely resembles their current tour guide, either the seventh or eighth generation direct descendants still in residence. You have the thousands of cousins gathering for Stirling family reunions at Wakefield Plantation, and at Catalpa Plantation you have the memories of the famous Fort hospitality encompassing all the generations, from the enormous cast-iron sugar kettles full of crushed ice holding frosted silver julep cups for grown-up parties, to the sunburnt freckle-faced little girls sent out to picnic among the hydrangeas and drooping pink indigo blooms with baskets heavy-laden with fried chicken and tiny tarts of lemon or pecan, pink lemonade with real cherries, teacakes and fresh strawberries.

At the monthly luncheons of the Romeo Club, the ever-shrinking alumnae group from the town's first public school, you have unofficial historian Jimmy Murphey reminding the group of hearing the radio broadcast of President Roosevelt's declaration of war after the bombing of Pearl Harbor; just as clearly he recalls picking dewberries down along Bayou Sara and spying on Irma Bennett and Tiny Wade jitterbugging to "In the Mood," or Eudora Ard pulling a block of ice home from the ice house in a little red wagon so she could make homemade ice cream, or the downtown block where commerce was dominated by the five Vinci brothers, Sammy at the gas station, Tony at the grocery and Frank the butcher, Joe with the cafe' and 3-V Tourist Courts still open for business today, and Salvadore running the bar in front of the dancehall where Sheriff Teddy Martin threw his recurrent re-election celebrations.

At Grace Episcopal Church you have the same families, just different generations, sitting in the same pews as in the mid-1800's, and through the stained glass windows they can gaze, during the sermon's less scintillating moments, at all the preceding generations slumbering in the peaceful surrounding cemetery. At Afton Villa you have the glorious gardens surviving the disastrous house fire to greet each spring with a determined riot of color, while at Greenwood Plantation even the house has risen from the ashes renewed. And at The Myrtles, if you look closely enough and believe hard enough, you just might see one of the early residents peering back at you from the depths of the silver-streaked mirror.

Yes, the Past is present still, but over the years the original pioneering families have been joined by newcomers from all over, bringing an influx of fresh ideas and new visions. While many small

towns have downtown commercial districts, St. Francisville's downtown area over the years developed the wonderful combination of business and residential use which contributes to its continued vitality, so that as the shops close for the evening, the brick sidewalks come alive with dog-walkers and skateboarders and strollers chatting over picket fences with the porch-rockers and swing-sitters, and as dusk falls and the band tunes up at Magnolia Cafe', young families gather for food and fellowship while exuberant youngsters dance and carouse in the closest this

staid old English area gets to Cajun joie de vivre. The Past contributes to the present, certainly, but no longer dominates, and the spirit of St. Francisville looks forward as enthusiastically as it looks back.

A Magical Place

Where the fertile rolling fields once were lush with cash crops like indigo and cotton, cane and corn and cattle, soybeans and sweet potatoes, now the area cultivates mostly historical and ecotourists, with an impact far beyond the financial. When we tend to take for granted the scenic surroundings to which we've grown accustomed, it sometimes takes an enthralled outsider's wonder at the area's un-spoiled treasures to reawaken our own appreciation. As the wise leaders of the local historical society have preached for years, our spring pilgrimage tours have as much to say to us as to our visitors, and finally we have gotten the message. This is a magical place, and we must treasure it and appreciate it and preserve it.

107

Trying to understand particular places and their importance in particular times, past chroniclers of history have taken many approaches, from paintings to plays, from diaries and journals to memoirs and poems, and volumes and volumes of books both fact and fiction. By combining images with words in this book, a labor of love, we hope we have captured just a bit of the magic of St. Francisville, its soul, its heart, its spirit, its timeless charm that is only enhanced by the patina of the passing of years, preserved on paper for posterity.

Observations of an adopted son...

Although I was raised from my youth in the plantation country of South Louisiana, like so many of us, I would pass right by my heritage without a second thought. Only after seeing through the lens of my camera did I begin to appreciate and understand those unique qualities that make this state and its little communities so magical. St. Francisville is the most magical of them all.

I can still recall a mysterious sensation racing through my soul the first time I crossed the Mississippi River into this "happy land." Alice must have felt the same when she discovered her "wonderland." Little did I know that I was about to become possessed by the Spirit of St. Francisville.

Perhaps by an accident or by some guiding force, I turned through the gates and down the oak-lined avenue to Butler Greenwood Plantation. That turn provided the inspiration for this book. At Butler Greenwood I found the Spirit of St. Francisville condensed into one special old homestead begun in the 1790s and still owned by the original family. Butler Greenwood exudes the essence of this community, its past and its present.

The majestic oaks, the blazing azaleas, the dazzling camellias and the delightful aromas of sweet olive and wisteria are enough to make a bird burst out in song. And the home, seated in the midst of this beauty like a king on his throne reminds everyone that the past still lives.

I found the Spirit of St. Francisville not just in this magnificent setting but also in those who reside or are employed at this one single old plantation. This spirit could not be any more evident than in the plantation owner, Anne Butler. Her incredible choice of words have made my images come to life. Only a gifted writer with a long-time insider's understanding of this place and its people could so tenderly describe this "happy land". I will forever be grateful to my dear friend. You see, Butler Greenwood is the complete package...it is the Spirit of St. Francisville.

My wife Nona and I have enjoyed the hospitality there many times, but each time the magic is just as strong. As I bring in visiting artists and photographers for the work-shops I conduct, these professionals from around the globe never fail to feel the same impact. I know my life will never be the same after having once traveled through the gate and down the path to the big house.

Darrell Chitty